M. L. A. (Mary

Five-o'-clock Tea

Victorian afternoon tea recipes

Including cakes, macaroons, savoury sandwiches and beverages.

JEPPESTOWN

Also available from Jeppestown Press

Where the Lion Roars: An 1890 African Colonial Cookery Book

The Bulawayo Cookery Book and Household Guide

The Anglo-African Who's Who 1907

Matabeleland and the Victoria Falls

With Captain Stairs to Katanga

The Ghana Cookery Book

Cooking in West Africa

The Imperial African Cookery Book

www.jeppestown.com

M. L. A. (Mary L. Allen)

Five-o'-clock Tea

Victorian afternoon tea recipes

JEPPESTOWN

Cover design copyright © Jeppestown Press 2011
Arrangement and index copyright © Jeppestown Press 2011
Back cover photo *Tea sandwiches at the Empress* courtesy of Robin
Zebrowski – see more pictures at http://www.flickr.com/photos/firepile

First published 1886 by Kegan Paul, Trench & Co. This edition
published 2011 by Jeppestown Press, London.
www.jeppestown.com

ISBN 978-0-9553936-9-3

All Rights Reserved. No part of this publication may be reproduced,
stored in a retrieval system, or transmitted, in any form or by any means,
electronic, mechanical, photocopying, recording, scanning or otherwise,
except as described below, without the permission in writing of the
Publisher. Copying is not permitted except for personal use, to the
extent permitted by national copyright law. Requests for permission for
other kinds of copying, such as copying for general distribution, for
advertising or promotional purposes, for creating new collective works, or
for resale, and other enquiries, should be addressed to the Publisher.

This is a facsimile of an original Victorian work and may consequently
have some faults resulting from the reproduction of the original text.

(The rights of translation and of reproduction are reserved.)

PREFACE.

THE great and unexpected success that has attended the publication of "Breakfast Dishes" and "Savouries and Sweets," induces me to offer to the public the present collection of receipts for that favourite meal known as "Five-o'clock Tea."

Now that the marriage hours have been extended to the afternoon, the old heavy "wedding-breakfast" will shortly be a thing of the past, and its place usurped by refreshments of a lighter and less expensive character, in view of which I have supplemented my English and Foreign cake receipts, with several for "Savoury Sandwiches," "Cups," "Cooling Drinks," etc., suitable for the purpose, and such as have been of late extensively used at afternoon teas in large establishments where the dinner hour is protracted beyond eight o'clock.

It may not be out of place here to say a few words about the order of mixing the ingredients of a cake; and if the directions given both here and in the receipts are implicitly followed, even the veriest amateur who tries her hand at cake making for the first time need not despair of success. As a rule, then, the ingredients for a cake should be mixed in the following order.

1. Butter and finely pounded and sifted sugar beaten together to a cream.

2. The well-whipped eggs.

3. The flour, added gradually while the beating continues.

4. Whatever else is to be put into the cake.

Baking tins should always be well greased with fresh butter before the cake mixture is poured into them, and the tins lined with well-greased paper.

If there is any fear of a cake burning on the top, a piece of greased paper should be laid over the tin.

If it is feared that the bottom heat of an oven is too fierce, the cake mould should be stood on a reversed baking tin.

The oven door should not be opened for half an hour after a cake is put in to bake, else the cake will become heavy.

To ascertain if a cake is sufficiently baked, a

clean knife should be run through the thickest part of it, and if, on withdrawal, none of the mixture is found adhering to it, the cake is done.

Directly a cake is baked, it should be turned out of its mould and placed out of all draught on its side on a sieve.

In conclusion, I may add that, as the present selection of receipts comprises many economical ones—notably, No. 12, Seed Cake; and No. 8, Chantry Sponge Cake; as well as those of a richer and more extravagant description, as No. 6, Chocolate Cake; No. 20, A Russian Cake; or No. 30, A Bride Cake;—this little handbook to "Five-o'Clock Tea" will be found equally useful for all degrees of society.

M. L. A.

CONTENTS.

NO.		PAGE
1.	Tea	1
2.	Coffee	2
3.	Cocoa	3
4.	Buttered Toast	4
5.	Bread and Butter, or Bread and Devonshire Cream	5
6.	Chocolate Cake	6
7.	Vanilla Soft Icing for Cakes	7
8.	The Chantry Sponge Cake	8
9.	Guernsey Pound Cake	9
10.	Chocolate Cake Drops	10
11.	Blitz Kuchen	11
12.	Seed Cake	12
13.	Rock Cakes	13
14.	Raisin Cake	14
15.	Cocoanut Macaroons	15
16.	Godrich Cakes	16
17.	Rolph Tea Cake	17
18.	Blay Nuts	18
19.	Gingerbread Nuts	19
20.	Baba, a Russian Cake	20

CONTENTS.

NO.		PAGE
21.	German Mandeln Cake	21
22.	Kaffee Brod	22
23.	Sweet S Tea Cakes	23
24.	Colne Tea Cakes	24
25.	Sugar Cakes	25
26.	Drop Cakes	26
27.	Chocolate Sponge Sandwiches—Chocolate Icing	27
28.	A Rich Currant Cake	28
29.	Cupid's Cakes	29
30.	Bride Cake	30
31.	Icing for Cakes	31
32.	Sweet Tea Buns	32
33.	Canadian Tea Cakes	33
34.	Currant Buns	34
35.	Huron Cakes	35
36.	Silver Cake	36
37.	Gold Cake	37
38.	Soft Golden Icing	38
39.	Windsor Castle Pound Cake	39
40.	Windsor Castle Rice Cake	40
41.	American Sweet Cakes	41
42.	Lemon Biscuits	42
43.	Short Bread	43
44.	Grandmother's Biscuits	44
45.	Farmhouse Cake	45
46.	Macaroons	46
47.	Madeira Cake	47
48.	Surrey Tea Cakes	48
49.	Queen's Sponge Cakes	49
50.	Small Sponge Cakes	50

CONTENTS.

NO.		PAGE
51.	Gingerbread	51
52.	Russian Walnut Cake	52
53.	Lobster Mayonnaise Sandwiches	53
54.	Nasturtium Leaves Sandwiches	55
55.	Tomato and Sardine Sandwiches	56
56.	Dried Salmon Sandwiches	57
57.	Caviare Sandwiches	58
58.	Shrimp Sandwiches	59
59.	Salsify Sandwiches	60
60.	Pâté de Foie Gras Sandwiches	61
61.	Asparagus Sandwiches	62
62.	Potted Salmon Sandwiches	63
63.	Mushroom Sandwiches	64
64.	Olive and Anchovy Sandwiches	65
65.	Egg and Gherkin Sandwiches	66
66.	Colnbrook Sandwiches	67
67.	Indian Ham Sandwiches	68
68.	Anchovy Sandwiches	69
69.	Tomato Sandwiches	70
70.	Thunder and Lightning Sandwiches	71
71.	Claret Cup	72
72.	Cider Cup	73
73.	Hock Cup	74
74.	Champagne Cup	74
75.	Sam Ward Kümmel	75
76.	Silver Fiz	75
77.	Iced Coffee	76
78.	Iced Tea and Lemon	76
79.	Lemon Syrup	77
80.	Lemonade	78
81.	Samson	78

FIVE-O'CLOCK TEA.

No. 1.—TEA.

Average cost of tea for eight persons, nine teaspoonfuls of tea at 3*s*. a lb., 8*d*.

1. Fill a kettle three-quarters full of fresh soft water and put it on to the fire to boil.

2. Heat the teapot before putting in the tea; but on no account pour hot water into it, as it should be thoroughly dry when the tea is introduced.

3. Put in the tea, a teaspoonful for each person, and one over.

4. Be sure that the water boils before pouring it, over the tea, into the teapot.

5. Allow the tea to draw for six minutes, but no longer, and serve.

No. 2.—COFFEE.

A good mixture for ordinary use is half Mocha and half Plantation, at 2s. a lb. Coffee should be roasted at home and ground only a few minutes before it is used.

1. Place a kettle of fresh soft water on the fire to boil.

2. Grind the coffee and allow an ounce for each person.

3. Place a thick, pointed calico bag in the percolator, put the ground coffee into it, and pour very slowly a quart of fast-boiling water. It must on no account be urged to run through quicker than it naturally would, as the brightness and clearness of the coffee depend on this.

4. After the water has all run through the percolator it should be allowed to simmer a few minutes, but on no account boil.

N.B.—The milk served with coffee must be boiling, and the cups filled two-thirds with it before the coffee is added.

No. 3.—COCOA.

(Van Houten's.)

Bought in tins, 3s. 9d. a lb. Two teaspoonfuls to be used for a breakfast cup.

1. Put the cocoa into an enamel-lined saucepan and mix it thoroughly with a little warm milk.
2. Place the saucepan on the fire and add half a pint of cold water for two teaspoonfuls of cocoa.
3. Let it boil up.
4. Half fill the cups with cocoa.
5. Add hot (but not boiled) milk to each, and a lump of sugar, if liked.
6. Serve at once.

N.B.—Van Houten's cocoa is so frequently ordered by physicians for dyspeptic and nervous patients, to be drank instead of tea, that a receipt showing how to prepare it will not be out of place in these pages.

No. 4.—BUTTERED TOAST.

Ingredients.

1 tin loaf
Salt butter.

1. Cut your slices of bread half an inch thick, and toast on both sides before a clear fire.

2. Put in a plate, butter thickly, and cut the crust off each slice.

3. The toast should be put in the oven a few minutes before being served, and sent to table in a hot muffin dish. The pieces of toast should be no larger than two inches and a half square.

N.B.—A delicate, thin square of toast spread with fresh dripping is by no means to be despised, and indeed is extensively ordered by doctors for persons suffering from dyspepsia and other disorders. A little salt sprinkled over the dripping is a great improvement.

No. 5.—BREAD and BUTTER or BREAD and DEVONSHIRE CREAM.

Ingredients.

White or
Brown bread,
Fresh butter or
Devonshire cream,
And a pinch of salt.

1. Take a tin loaf a day old, cut off the outside crust.

2. If the butter to be used is hard, warm it before the fire.

3. Spread it on the bread with a large sharp knife.

4. Cut the bread as thin as possible, taking care it does not break.

5. Lay the slices evenly on a plate, or roll up each slice neatly and place in rows.

6. Serve, if liked, alternate slices of white and brown bread and butter on the same plate.

No. 6.—CHOCOLATE CAKE.

Average Cost.

Ingredients.

	s.	d.
½ lb. of almonds	1	0
½ lb. of sifted sugar	0	2
½ lb. of chocolate	0	6
9 eggs	0	9
2 oz. of bread crumbs	0	1
3 drops of vanilla	0	1
	2	7

Time required, from one hour to one hour and a half.

1. Put the yolks of nine eggs in a clean basin, and beat them to a cream with a fork.

2. Add by degrees half a pound of grated chocolate.

3. Then half a pound of castor sugar, sifted.

4. Blanch the almonds and chop small; add them to the other ingredients.

5. Mix a few drops of vanilla.

6. Stir in two ounces of sifted bread crumbs.

7. Mix all well together.

8. Beat the whites of five eggs to a snow, and stir lightly into the other ingredients.

9. Butter a mould or tin, well sprinkle with bread crumbs, and put the cake mixture into it.

10. Bake in a moderate oven.

11. When baked, a little white sugar should be shaken over this cake, or it can be iced in the following manner with vanilla icing.

No. 7.—VANILLA SOFT ICING FOR CHOCOLATE CAKE.

Average Cost.

Ingredients.

	s.	d.
½ a teaspoonful of essence of vanilla	0	1
2 teaspoonfuls of boiling water.		
½ lb. of sugar	0	2½
	0	3½

1. Mix the essence of vanilla with three teaspoonfuls of boiling water in an enamel-lined saucepan.

2. Let it boil up.

3. Have ready half a pound of finely sifted and pounded white sugar.

4. Mix it with the boiling water and vanilla.

5. Spread it on the top of the cake.

6. Stand it in a cool place to dry.

No. 8.—THE CHANTRY SPONGE CAKE.

Average Cost.

Ingredients.

		s.	d.
½ lb. of flour...		0	1
¾ lb. of lump sugar		0	2
¾ of a cup of boiling water.			
7 eggs		0	9
		1	0

Time required for baking, one hour and a half.

1. Melt three-quarters of a pound of sugar in a little water.

2. Beat the yolks of seven eggs and the whites of four together.

3. Mix with the above three parts of a cup of boiling water.

4. Dredge into the other ingredients half a pound of flour.

5. Beat all together for twenty minutes.

6. Pour into a well-buttered cake tin, and bake in a moderate oven.

No. 9.—GUERNSEY POUND CAKE.

AVERAGE COST.

Ingredients.

	s.	d.
½ lb. of flour	0	1
½ lb. of butter	0	9
½ lb. of sifted sugar	0	1
6 eggs	0	8
	1	7

Time required, about one hour.

1. Beat the yolks of six eggs in a clean basin.
2. Beat the whites of six eggs in a clean basin.
3. Cream the butter, add it to the beaten eggs.
4. Dredge in slowly the mixed flour and sugar.
5. Mix all the ingredients lightly, and beat the cake for half an hour.
6. Pour into a well-greased cake tin, and bake in a quick oven.

No. 10.—CHOCOLATE CAKE DROPS.

Average Cost.

Ingredients.

	s.	d.
¼ lb. of powdered chocolate	0	6
¼ lb. of sifted sugar	0	0¾
3 eggs	0	4
	0	10¾

Time, about ten minutes.

1. Beat the whites of three eggs to a stiff froth.

2. Mix a quarter of a pound of chocolate, and a quarter of a pound of sifted white sugar.

3. Stir in the whites of the beaten eggs lightly with a fork.

4. Drop on a buttered tin with a teaspoon, and bake in a slow oven.

No. 11.—BLITZ KUCHEN.

Average Cost.

Ingredients.

	s.	d.
1 lb. of lump sugar	0	2½
1 lemon	0	1½
10 eggs	0	10
¾ lb. of flour	0	2
2 oz. of butter	0	4
	1	8

Time, about one hour.

1. Beat the yolks of ten eggs.
2. Stir them by degrees into a pound of finely pounded and sifted white sugar.
3. Stir for half an hour after they are all added.
4. Dissolve two ounces of butter in an enamelled pan; let it be warm, but not hot.
5. Add to it the grated rind of a small lemon,
6. And three-quarters of a pound of fine flour.
7. Mix all well together.
8. Stir in lightly the stiff snow of the whites of ten eggs.
9. Butter a cake tin with fresh butter, and strew it with powdered bread crumbs.
10. Bake in a hot oven.

N.B.—The tin for *baking a lightning cake* should be flat, four inches high, and nearly a foot in circumference.

No. 12.—SEED CAKE.

Average Cost.

Ingredients.

	s.	d.
½ lb. of butter	0	8
½ lb. of sugar	0	1¾
1 lb. of flour	0	2¼
¼ oz. of caraway seeds	0	0½
1 lemon	0	1
3 eggs	0	3
1 teaspoonful of baking powder	0	1
	1	5½

Time required, one hour and a half.

1. Beat three eggs well.

2. Beat half a pound of butter in a basin with half a pound of pounded loaf sugar until it creams.

3. Mix the baking powder well into the flour.

4. Add this to the butter and sugar.

5. Mix with it the grated rind of a lemon, and the caraway seeds.

6. Stir into the whole a gill of milk.

7. Line a tin with buttered paper, put in the cake mixture, and bake in a moderate oven.

No. 13.—ROCK CAKES.

AVERAGE COST.

Ingredients.

	s.	d.
½ lb. of butter	0	8
½ lb. of flour	0	1½
½ lb. of moist sugar	0	1¾
½ lb. of currants	0	3
2 eggs	0	2
40 drops of essence of lemon	0	1
½ glass of brandy	0	4
	1	9¼

Time required, half an hour

1. Put the flour into a clean basin.
2. Rub the butter well into it.
3. Mix in the moist sugar thoroughly.
4. Add the well-washed and dry currants.
5. Also the essence of lemon.
6. Beat two eggs well.
7. Add the brandy to them.
8. Stir the whole of the ingredients together.
9. With a spoon drop the mixture in lumps on a baking sheet.
10. Bake in a moderate oven.

No. 14.—RAISIN CAKE.

Average Cost.

Ingredients.		s.	d.
1 lb. of flour		0	2¼
1 lb. of sugar		0	4
1 lb. of butter		1	4
1 lb. of raisins		0	6
6 eggs		0	6
1 glass of brandy		0	6
½ a small nutmeg		0	1
1 teaspoonful of carbonate of soda ...		0	0½

Time, one hour and a half.   3   5¾

1. Beat the yolks of six eggs well.

2. Whip the whites to a stiff froth.

3. Beat a pound of butter in a basin till it creams.

4. Add to the butter one pound of sugar that has been pounded.

5. Also the flour.

6. Stir in the yolks of eggs.

7. Add the glass of brandy to the above, and

8. The nutmeg.

9. Dissolve the soda in a tablespoonful of hot water.

10. Stir into the other ingredients.

11. Beat all together until the whole is light and creamy.

12. Strew a cupful of flour over the chopped stoned raisins, to prevent them from sticking together.

13. Stir them into the cake mixture.

14. Whisk in lightly the whites of eggs.

15. Line a tin with buttered paper, and bake in quick oven.

No. 15.—COCOANUT MACAROONS.

AVERAGE COST.

Ingredients.

	s.	d.
½ lb. of cocoanut	0	6
1 lb. of sugar	0	4
8 eggs	0	8
	1	6

Time required, twenty minutes.

1. Grate some fresh cocoanut, spread it on a dish, and allow it to dry gradually for twenty-four hours.

2. Add to it one pound of finely pounded and sifted sugar.

3. Beat the whites of eight eggs to a stiff solid froth.

4. Mix lightly into the cocoanut and sugar.

5. When thoroughly mixed, put in round lumps on a buttered tin.

6. Bake in a moderate oven, on the shelf nearest the top.

7. Move the cakes from the tin while they are warm, and store them in a dry canister as soon as cool.

No. 16.—GODRICH CAKES.

AVERAGE COST OF ABOUT SIX.

Ingredients.

		s.	d.
5 oz. of flour	...	0	1½
¾ oz. of butter	...	0	1
5 oz. of sugar	...	0	1¼
1 teaspoonful of baking powder	...	0	0½
4 eggs	...	0	4
A few drops of vanilla	...	0	0½
		0	8¾

Time, fifteen to twenty minutes.

1. Into a clean basin put five ounces of sifted flour.

2. Rub into it three-quarters of an ounce of butter

3. Mix five ounces of finely pounded loaf sugar,

4. And one teaspoonful of baking powder.

5. Beat up four eggs, the yolks and whites separately.

6. Mix with the yolks six tablespoonfuls of cold water

7. Flavour with a few drops of vanilla.

8. Mix all the ingredients well together.

9. Divide into little cakes, and bake in patty tins in a moderate oven.

No. 17.—ROLPH TEA CAKE.

AVERAGE COST.

Ingredients.

	s.	d.
1 lb. of flour	0	2¼
1 teaspoonful of baking powder	0	0½
2 oz. of butter	0	2
2 eggs	0	2
¾ oz. of sugar	0	0½
½ a gill of milk	0	0½
A sprinkling of salt.		
	0	7¾

Time, half an hour.

1. Put one pound of flour into a clean basin.
2. Rub two ounces of butter into the flour,
3. And one teaspoonful of baking powder.
4. Put in a sprinkling of salt.
5. Mix in three-quarters of an ounce of pounded sugar.
6. Beat two eggs well with half a gill of milk.
7. Mix with the rest of the ingredients.
8. Beat all well up together.
9. Bake in a cake tin in a moderate oven.
10. When done cut up into thick slices.
11. Butter liberally and serve very hot.

No. 18.—BLAY NUTS.

Average Cost.

Ingredients.

	s.	d.
2 oz. of butter	0	2
6 oz. of flour	0	1½
2 oz. of sugar	0	0½
1 egg	0	1
¼ of a pot of apricot jam	0	3
½ a gill of milk	0	0½
	0	8½

Time, to be boiled for from ten to fifteen minutes.

1. Put six ounces of flour into a clean basin.
2. Rub into it two ounces of butter.
3. Then two ounces of pounded sugar.
4. Beat one egg with half a gill of milk.
5. Mix with the other ingredients into a thick paste.
6. Cut into pieces.
7. Roll out.
8. Put a little apricot jam into the middle of each.
9. Roll up into balls, about the size of a billiard ball.
10. Have ready some boiling lard.
11. Boil the balls in it from ten to fifteen minutes.
12. When done and a nice brown, take out, drain, and roll in pounded sugar.
13. Serve either hot or cold.

No. 19.—GINGERBREAD NUTS.

Average Cost.

Ingredients.

	s.	d.
1½ lb. of flour	0	3¾
½ lb. of butter	0	8
½ lb. of sugar	0	1½
1 lb. of treacle	0	2½
¾ oz. of ginger	0	1½
A sprinkling of pepper		
	1	5¼

Time, about half-an-hour.

1. Put one pound and a half of flour into a clean basin.

2. Rub into it half a pound of butter,

3. And three-quarters of an ounce of ground ginger.

4. Warm one pound of treacle and half a pound of moist sugar.

5. Sprinkle a little pepper on the dry ingredients.

6. Mix everything thoroughly together to a stiff dough.

7. Roll into flat thin paste.

8. Cut out into biscuits with a cutter.

9. Bake on a flat floured tin in a quick oven.

No. 20.—BABA, A RUSSIAN CAKE.

Average Cost.

Ingredients.		s.	d.
1½ lb. of flour	...	0	3¾
2 oz. of butter	...	0	2
5 eggs	...	0	5
½ lb. of sugar	...	0	2
1 lemon	...	0	1
1 pint of milk	...	0	2
¼ lb. of almonds	...	0	4
¾ oz. of German yeast	...	0	1
A few drops of rose water.			
		1	8¾

Time for baking, one hour.

1. Dissolve the yeast in a pint of milk.

2. Put three-quarters of a pound of flour into a basin.

3. Mix well with it the dissolved yeast and milk.

4. Put the mixture in a warm place to rise for one hour

5. Blanch a quarter of a pound of almonds.

6. Pound them in a mortar with a few drops of rose water and a little sugar.

7. Beat two ounces of butter to a cream.

8. Beat the yolks of five eggs.

9. When the dough is risen sufficiently, add the butter, eggs, almonds, and the grated rind of a small lemon.

10. Then the half-pound of pounded sugar, and

11. Three-quarters of a pound more of flour.

12. Beat the mixture well, and pour it in a tin that has been buttered and strewn with bread crumbs.

13. Bake in a moderate oven.

No. 21.—GERMAN MANDELN CAKE.

AVERAGE COST.

Ingredients.	s.	d.
½ lb. of fresh butter	0	8
4 oz. of sweet almonds	0	6
1 oz. of bitter almonds	0	2
9 eggs	0	9
¾ lb. of flour	0	1¾
3 dessert-spoonfuls of brewer's yeast	0	0½
1 tumbler of milk	0	1
A few bread crumbs.		
¾ lb. of white pounded sugar	0	3½
	2	7¾

Time, about one hour and a quarter.

1. Peel, blanch, and pound the sweet and bitter almonds with a little milk till quite fine.
2. Pound and sift three-quarters of a pound of loaf sugar.
3. Mix it with the almonds.
4. Break nine eggs.
5. Beat the yolks well,
6. And the whites to a stiff froth.
7. To the yolks, sugar, and almonds, add three-quarters of a pound of flour, a pinch of salt,
8. And three dessert-spoonfuls of yeast.
9. Also a tumbler of tepid milk.
10. Beat the mixture quite smooth.
11. Stir in lightly the stiff frothed whites of eggs.
12. Pour the whole into a buttered tin, sprinkled with very finely powdered bread crumbs.
13. Put the cake in a warm place to rise, and, when it has risen to half its size, put it in a hot oven.
14. When cold, strew the cake with white sifted sugar.

No. 22.—KAFFEE BROD—COFFEE CAKES.

Average Cost.

Ingredients.

		s.	d.
1 pint of new milk	...	0	2
8 oz. of fresh butter	...	0	8
6 oz. of white sugar	...	0	1¾
½ lb. of flour	...	0	1
2 dessert-spoonfuls of rose-water	...	0	1
9 eggs	...	0	9
		1	10¾

Time, about twenty minutes.

1. Boil one pint of new milk with eight ounces of butter and six ounces of white sugar.

2. Add, while the milk is boiling, half a pound of flour, and

3. Two dessert-spoonfuls of rose-water.

4. Stir over the fire till perfectly smooth.

5. Empty the dough from the enamelled saucepan into a basin.

6. At once stir in the well-beaten yolks of nine eggs,

7. And the whites of seven.

8. Butter a baking tin.

9. Place the dough on it in rows, in little heaps (formed by using a dessert-spoon).

10. Brush the tops over with a little white of an egg.

11. Strew a little sugar over also, and bake in a moderate oven.

No. 23.—SWEET S TEA CAKES.

AVERAGE COST.

Ingredients.

	s.	d.
½ lb. of flour	0	1
¼ lb. of white sugar	0	1¼
3 eggs	0	3
6 oz. of butter	0	7
	1	0¼

Time, about twenty minutes.

1. Beat the yolks of three eggs.
2. Mix them with the flour and white pounded sugar.
3. Heat the fresh butter and beat it to a cream.
4. Add the rest of the ingredients gradually to the butter.
5. Mix the dough thoroughly well.
6. Roll it out.
7. Cut it into strips five inches long.
8. Twist each strip into the shape of an S.
9. Brush each one over with white of egg slightly sugared.
10. Place on a baking tin in a moderate oven.

No. 24.—COLNE TEA CAKES.

Average Cost.

Ingredients.

		s.	d.
1¾ lb. of flour	...	0	3
2 oz. of sugar	...	0	0½
2 oz. of butter	...	0	2
2 eggs	...	0	2
1 oz. of German yeast	...	0	1½
½ pint of milk	...	0	1
		0	10

N.B.—This quantity will make two cakes.

1. Put the flour into a basin.
2. Dissolve the German yeast in a little milk.
3. Mix it into the flour.
4. Then mix in the pounded sugar.
5. Warm the butter in half a pint of milk.
6. Put a little salt into the warm milk.
7. Well beat the eggs.
8. Mix all the ingredients together.
9. Put the mixture in a greased tin.
10. Let the tin stand in a warm place for the dough to rise for one hour.
11. Bake in cake tins or rings.
12. When done, cut into slices, and butter the cakes hot.

No. 25.—SUGAR CAKES (DELICIOUS).

Average Cost.

Ingredients.

	s.	d.
1 lb. of flour	0	2½
½ lb. of sugar	0	2
½ lb. of butter	0	8
2 eggs	0	2
1 lemon	0	1
	1	3¼

Time, about a quarter of an hour.

1. Take a clean basin and put into it one pound of flour.

2. Rub the butter into the flour,

3. And the grated rind of a large lemon.

4. Mix with the whole half a pound of pounded sugar.

5. Beat two eggs well.

6. Mix all the ingredients together,

7. Roll out thin.

8. Cut the cakes out with a biscuit cutter.

9. Place on a well-buttered baking tin, and bake in a moderate oven.

No. 26.—DROP CAKES.

Average Cost.

Ingredients.

		s.	d.
1 lb. of flour	...	0	2¼
½ lb. of butter	...	0	8
½ lb. of sugar	...	0	2
2 eggs	...	0	2
1 lemon	...	0	1
¼ lb. of currants	...	0	1½
		1	4¾

Time, from a quarter to half an hour.

1. Put the flour into a basin.
2. Rub the butter into the flour.
3. Mix in the pounded sugar.
4. Grate the lemon peel.
5. Mix it into the other things.
6. Wash and well dry the currants.
7. Beat the eggs well.
8. Mix all together.
9. Flour a baking sheet.
10. Drop the mixture on to it in lumps.
11. Bake in a moderate oven.

No. 27.—CHOCOLATE SPONGE SANDWICHES.

AVERAGE COST.

Ingredients.		s.	d.
3 eggs	...	0	3
3 oz. of sugar	...	0	0¾
4 oz. of flour	...	0	1
1 lemon	...	0	1
		0	5¾

CHOCOLATE ICING.

		s.	d.
2 eggs	...	0	2
¼ lb. of sugar	...	0	1
3 oz. of chocolate	...	0	3
		0	6

1. Put into a basin six ounces of finely pounded sugar.

2. Break three eggs into the sugar and beat for three-quarters of an hour.

3. Add the grated rind of half a lemon.

4. Mix in well four ounces of flour, and

5. Bake immediately on a flat tin lined with paper.

6. When done, turn it over and wet the paper a little with a pastry brush to get it off.

7. Spread half the surface with apricot jam.

8. Use the remaining half for the top of the sandwich.

9. For icing, beat the whites of two eggs to a stiff froth.

10. Melt the chocolate in a saucepan with a little water, and mix it with the sugar.

11. Stir into it the white froth of the beaten eggs when cool.

12. Spread the chocolate mixture over the top of the sandwiches.

13. Cut into any shapes that are liked.

No. 28.—A RICH CURRANT CAKE.

Average Cost.

Ingredients.

		s.	d.
1 lb. of flour		0	2¼
½ lb. of butter		0	8
½ pint of milk		0	1
½ lb. of sugar		0	2
2 eggs		0	2
½ lb. of currants		0	3
¼ lb. of peel		0	3
		1	9¼

Time, one hour.

1. Take a clean basin and put one pound of flour into it.

2. Rub half a pound of butter into the flour.

3. Well wash, pick, and dry the currants.

4. Mix half a pound of pounded sugar with them,

5. And a quarter of a pound of mixed candied lemon and orange peel.

6. Also half a teaspoonful of grated nutmeg.

7. Beat two eggs well in half a pint of milk.

8. Mix all the ingredients thoroughly together.

9. Bake in a buttered tin in a moderate oven.

No. 29.—CUPID'S CAKES.

Average Cost.

Ingredients.		s.	d.
½ oz. of yeast		0	1½
4 eggs		0	4
1½ lb. of flour		0	3¼
1 lb. of butter		1	4
½ lb. of sugar		0	2
½ a pint of milk		0	1
¼ lb. of candied peel		0	3
		2	6¾

Time, according to size.

1. Take a clean basin.
2. Put into it one pound and a half of flour.
3. Make a hollow in the centre.
4. Beat up four eggs.
5. Dissolve half an ounce of yeast in a cup of water.
6. Add it and half a pint of new milk to the eggs.
7. Pour the mixture into the flour.
8. Stir all together into a dough.
9. Work it well.
10. Melt one pound of butter, but do not make it hot.
11. Add it by degrees to the dough.
12. Thoroughly knead it.
13. Put the dough in a warm place to rise for one hour.
14. After it has risen, mix with the dough half a pound of pounded sugar.
15. Bake in small cake tins previously buttered.
16. Ornament the top of each cake with cut candied peel.
17. Bake in a moderate oven.

No. 30.—BRIDE CAKE.

AVERAGE COST.

Ingredients.	s.	d.
1 lb. of butter	1	4
1 lb. of flour	0	2½
1 lb. of sugar	0	4
4 lb. of currants	2	0
12 eggs	1	0
2 lb. of candied citron and lemon peel	1	6
1 lb. of almonds	2	4
2 nutmegs	0	4½
¼ pint of rum	0	6
	9	7

Time, four to five hours.

1. Beat one pound of butter till it creams in
2. One pound of brown sugar.
3. Mix well.
4. Beat the twelve eggs well.
5. Beat again thoroughly with the butter and sugar.
6. Add the pound of flour.
7. Well mix with the other ingredients.
8. Wash, pick, and dry four pounds of currants.
9. Add them to the flour, etc.
10. Blanch, dry, and chop one pound of almonds.
11. Add it, with the two pounds of candied peel, to the cake.
12. Grate two nutmegs, and mix all together.
13. Add the quarter of a pint of rum.
14. Beat all the ingredients well together.
15. Bake in a tin lined with buttered paper
16. In a moderate oven.

No. 31.—ICING FOR CAKES.

Average Cost.

Ingredients.

	s.	d.
4 eggs	0	4
1 lb. of icing sugar	1	6
	1	10

1. Beat the whites of the eggs to a stiff froth with a wooden spoon, having been very careful that no particle of yolk gets among them.

2. Roll the icing sugar and sift it through a fine sieve.

3. Mix the sugar gradually with the eggs.

4. Work the two together for a few minutes and add a drop or two of vanilla essence.

5. Now spread it smoothly over the cake to be iced.

6. Dry it very gently indeed, in quite a cool oven.

N.B.—Should the icing be required of a pink colour, use a drop or two of cochineal, and thoroughly mix it with the icing before spreading it over the surface of the cake. From the difference in the size of eggs, a little more or less sugar may be required.

No. 32.—SWEET TEA BUNS.

Average Cost.

Ingredients.

	s.	d.
½ lb. of sugar..	0	2
¼ lb. of butter	0	4
6 oz. of flour	0	1
5 eggs	0	5
½ a teaspoonful of essence of vanilla	0	0½
	1	0½

Time, half to three-quarters of an hour.

1. Take a clean basin.
2. Beat in it a quarter of a pound of butter, and
3. Half a pound of pounded sugar till it creams.
4. Then mix in six ounces of flour thoroughly.
5. And the essence of vanilla to flavour it.
6. Beat the whites of five eggs to a stiff froth.
7. Lightly stir them into the other ingredients.
8. Bake in a flat tin that has been well buttered, in a moderate oven.
9. When partly cooked, cut into any shapes required.
10. To be eaten hot for afternoon tea.

No. 33.—CANADIAN TEA CAKES.

Average Cost.

Ingredients.	s.	d.
1 lb. of flour	0	2½
½ pint of milk	0	1
2 oz. of butter	0	2
¼ lb. of sugar	0	1
2 oz. of currants	0	0½
2 eggs	0	2
1 teaspoonful of baking powder	0	0½
	0	9½

Time, half an hour.

1. Take a clean basin.
2. Put one pound of flour into it.
3. Rub into the flour a heaped teaspoonful of baking powder.
4. Then rub in two ounces of butter.
5. Wash, pick, and dry two ounces of currants.
6. Add a quarter of a pound of pounded sugar, and
7. The currants to the other ingredients.
8. Well beat the two eggs with
9. Half a pint of milk.
10. Mix everything well together.
11. Flour a paste board.
12. Roll out the dough.
13. Form into tea cakes.
14. Bake on a buttered tin in a moderate oven.
15. When half done, wash over with the yolk of an egg beaten in a teaspoonful of milk.
16. Bake till done, then cut in slices and butter.
17. Serve hot.

No. 34.—CURRANT BUNS.

Average Cost.

Ingredients.

		s.	d.
1 lb. of flour	...	0	2¼
½ lb. of sugar	...	0	1
¼ lb. of butter	...	0	4
¼ lb. of currants	...	0	1½
½ pint of milk	...	0	1
3 teaspoonfuls of baking-powder	...	0	1
		0	10¾

Time, about half an hour.

1. Melt a quarter of a pound of butter in
2. Half a pint of milk, but do not let it get hot.
3. Put one pound of flour into a basin, and
4. Rub into it three teaspoonfuls of baking-powder.
5. A pinch of salt, and
6. Half a pound of moist sugar.
7. Mix into a dough with the butter and milk.
8. Wash and dry a quarter of a pound of currants.
9. Mix the currants with the other ingredients.
10. Divide the dough into small pieces.
11. Shape into buns.
12. Glaze with the yolk of an egg beaten up, applied with a pastry brush, before putting the buns in the oven.
13. Bake on a greased tin in a hot oven.

No. 35.—HURON CAKES.

Average Cost.

Ingredients.

	s.	*d.*
½ lb. of flour	0	1¼
½ lb. of butter	0	4
1 egg	0	1
2 tablespoonfuls of sour cream ...	0	2
6 oz. of sugar	0	1½
¼ pot of apricot jam	0	4
	1	1¾

Time, about half an hour.

N.B.—These cakes are delicious without any jam in them, and more suitable for afternoon tea.

1. Beat a quarter of a pound of butter to a cream with
2. Six ounces of pounded loaf sugar.
3. Mix in half a pound of sifted flour.
4. Beat up one egg with
5. Two tablespoonfuls of sour cream.
6. Mix thoroughly with the other ingredients.
7. Roll out the paste.
8. Cut into three-cornered pieces.
9. Bake on a baking sheet in a hot oven.
10. When cold, put a lump of apricot jam in the middle of each cake.
11. Serve.

No. 36.—SILVER CAKE.

Average Cost.

Ingredients.

	s.	d.
½ lb. of white sugar	0	2
¼ lb. of butter	0	4
6 oz. of flour	0	1
5 eggs	0	5
40 drops of essence of almonds	0	2
	1	2

Time, three-quarters to one hour.

1. Beat a quarter of a pound of butter to a cream with

2. Half a pound of pounded loaf sugar.

3. Add six ounces of sifted flour.

4. Mix well.

5. Beat five whites of eggs to a stiff froth.

6. Stir lightly into the other things.

7. Flavour the cake with forty drops of essence of almonds.

8. Bake, in a hot oven at first, in a tin lined with buttered paper.

9. Cover the cake while warm with half a pound of vanilla icing (No. 7).

No. 37.—GOLD CAKE.

AVERAGE COST.

Ingredients.	s.	d.
¼ lb. of butter	0	4
½ lb. of sugar	0	2
½ lb. of flour	0	1¼
5 eggs	0	5
1 orange	0	1
1 lemon	0	1
¼ teaspoonful of carbonate of soda	0	0¼
½ a gill of milk	0	0¼
1 teaspoonful of vinegar	0	0¼
A very little ground mace	0	0¼
A few grains of turmeric	0	0¼
	1	3½

Bake three-quarters to one hour in an oven hot at first and slow afterwards.

1. Beat a quarter of a pound of butter with
2. Half a pound of finely powdered sugar until it creams.
3. Beat up the yolks of five eggs.
4. Mix them with half a pound of flour that has been coloured with the turmeric, and the other ingredients.
5. Then add a quarter of a teaspoonful of carbonate of soda dissolved in half a gill of milk.
6. Then mix in the strained juice of a lemon, in which the rind of an orange has been grated.
7. Also the vinegar and
8. The ground mace.
9. Bake in a tin lined with buttered paper. Ice the top with golden icing (No. 38).

No. 38.—SOFT GOLDEN ICING.

AVERAGE COST.

Ingredients.

	s.	d.
2 pinches of turmeric	0	0½
2 or 3 tablespoonfuls of water.		
1 lemon	0	1
1 lb. of loaf sugar	0	5½
	0	7

1. Strain the juice of a lemon, and mix it with

2. Two or three tablespoonfuls of water.

3. Add two pinches of turmeric powder.

4. Boil the water in a small enamelled saucepan.

5. Pound and sift a pound of loaf sugar.

6. With a wooden spoon mix the boiling turmeric-water with the sugar till quite smooth.

7. Spread the soft icing on the top and sides of the cake while it is yet hot.

8. Stand the cake on a sieve to cool in a place free from draughts.

No. 39.—WINDSOR CASTLE POUND CAKE.

AVERAGE COST.

Ingredients.

	s.	d.
1 lb. of butter	1	4
1 teaspoonful of baking powder	0	0½
1¼ lb. of best flour	0	4
1 lb. of loaf sugar	0	5
10 eggs	0	10
1 lemon	0	1
	3	0½

Time, about one hour to one hour and a half.

N.B.—This quantity will make two nice-sized cakes.

1. Work one pound of butter in a basin till it creams.
2. Add to it one pound of finely pounded loaf sugar.
3. Work all together for five minutes.
4. Beat ten eggs separately, and work one at a time into the paste till all are nicely mixed in with it.
5. Then add one pound and a quarter of best flour,
6. And the rind of a grated lemon.
7. Either a few ounces of well-washed currants, or a tablespoonful of caraway seeds.
8. Mix all the ingredients thoroughly together.
9. Bake in tins lined with buttered paper.

No. 40.—WINDSOR CASTLE RICE CAKE.

Average Cost.

Ingredients.

		s.	d.
½ lb. of butter	...	0	8
5 eggs ...	...	0	5
½ lb. of sugar	...	0	2½
¼ lb. of flour	...	0	1
6 oz. of ground rice	...	0	2½
2 oz. of candied peel or preserved ginger		0	1½
		1	8½

Time, one hour.

1. Take a clean basin, and beat in it half a pound of butter to a cream.

2. Mix into the butter half a pound of pounded loaf sugar.

3. Beat five eggs well.

4. Mix them with the other things.

5. Mix together the quarter of a pound of flour and six ounces of ground rice.

6. Add them to the other ingredients.

7. Mix thoroughly.

8. Add two ounces of preserved ginger, cut into dice, or candied peel, cut the same way.

9. Bake in a tin lined with buttered paper.

No. 41.—AMERICAN SWEET CAKES.

Average Cost.

Ingredients.

	s.	d.
1½ lb. of flour	0	3¼
1 lb. of sugar	0	5
1 lb. of butter	1	6
10 eggs	0	10
1 gill of orange flower water	0	3
1 lemon	0	1
½ a glass of brandy	0	4
	3	8¼

Time, from fifteen to twenty minutes.

1. Put one pound and a half of flour into a basin.
2. Mix with it one pound of finely powdered loaf sugar.
3. Then rub into it one pound of fresh butter.
4. Beat well ten eggs with
5. One gill of orange flower water, and
6. Half a glass of brandy.
7. Mix the whole of the ingredients together, and beat for half an hour.
8. Line some low square baking tins with buttered paper.
9. Put in the mixture about half an inch deep.
10. Bake in a quick oven.
11. When done, cut into squares or diamonds.
12. Ice while hot with vanilla or golden soft icing (Nos. 7 and 38).

No. 42.—LEMON BISCUITS.

Average Cost.

Ingredients.

		s.	d.
1½ lb. of flour	... ...	0	3½
¼ lb. of butter	... ...	0	4
1½ lb. of sugar	... ...	0	6
3 lemons...	... ...	0	3
2 eggs	... ...	0	2
		1	6½

Time, fifteen minutes.

1. Dry thoroughly before the fire one pound and a half of flour.

2. Then rub into it a quarter of a pound of butter as fine as possible.

3. Mix with it one pound and a half of pounded loaf sugar,

4. And the rind of three grated lemons.

5. Well beat two eggs.

6. Add to the beaten egg the juice of two lemons, and stir them thoroughly into each other.

7. Put the mixture into the flour, and mix together until you have a stiff paste.

8. Roll out the paste to the thickness of a penny piece.

9. Divide into biscuits with a paste cutter.

10. Bake on a baking sheet.

N.B.—These biscuits must be kept in a tin box near a fire till wanted, as they are apt to give.

No. 43.—SHORT BREAD.

AVERAGE COST.

Ingredients.

		s.	d.
½ lb. of butter	... ...	0	8
1 lb. of flour	... ...	0	2¼
4 oz. of castor sugar	... ...	0	1½
1 oz. of candied peel	... ...	0	1
		1	0¾

Time, about half an hour.

1. Put one pound of flour into a basin.
2. Warm and cream half a pound of butter.
3. Add four ounces of sugar to the flour,
4. As well as the creamed butter and candied peel, cut up small.
5. Mix thoroughly together.
6. Work the paste well.
7. Roll out the paste on a board.
8. Butter a flat baking tin.
9. Roll the paste until it is about half an inch thick.
10. Place it on the baking tin, and bake in a brisk oven. Serve cold.

No. 44.—GRANDMOTHER'S BISCUITS.

Average Cost.

Ingredients.

	s.	d.
1 lb. of sugar	0	4
1 lb. of butter	1	6
1 lb. of flour	0	2¼
2 eggs	0	2
	2	2¼

Time, about five minutes.

1. Warm one pound of butter in a saucepan.

2. Put one pound of flour into a clean basin.

3. Rub the butter into the flour.

4. Then mix in one pound of pounded loaf sugar.

5. Beat two eggs well.

6. Mix all together.

7. Flour a board, and put the paste on it.

8. Take a rolling-pin and flour it, roll out the paste very thin.

9. Flour a flat baking sheet.

10. Cut the paste into biscuits with a cutter.

11. Place on the tin, and bake in a moderate oven.

No. 45.—FARMHOUSE CAKE.

AVERAGE COST.

Ingredients.

	s.	d.
¾ lb. of flour	0	2
1 lb. of sugar	0	4
14 eggs	1	2
1 glass of sherry	0	6
	2	2

Time, one hour.

1. Put three-quarters of a pound of flour into a basin.

2. Add to it one pound of pounded and sifted loaf sugar.

3. Beat the yolks of fourteen eggs with a glass of sherry for half an hour.

4. Beat the whites of fourteen eggs to a stiff froth.

5. Stir lightly into the cake.

6. Line a tin with buttered paper.

7. Bake in a good oven.

No. 46.—MACAROONS.

Average Cost.

Ingredients.

		s.	d.
1 lb. of sweet almonds	... ...	1	2
1 lb. of sugar	...	0	4
6 eggs	...	0	6
1 gill of rose-water ...	...	0	0½
		2	0½

Time, about twenty minutes.

1. Blanch and pound one pound of sweet almonds in a mortar.

2. Put a gill of rose-water with the almonds to prevent them from oiling.

3. Take the pounded almonds out of the mortar, and put them into a clean basin.

4. Pound and sift one pound of loaf sugar.

5. Add it to the almonds in the basin.

6. Beat the whites of four eggs to a stiff froth.

7. Add them to the almonds and sugar.

8. Beat the whole lightly together.

9. Drop a tablespoonful of the mixture at a time on to some wafer paper placed on a flat (buttered) tin till it is covered.

10. Grate some sugar over the macaroons.

11. Bake in a moderately warm oven.

N.B.—The macaroons should be kept in a tin box.

No. 47.—MADEIRA CAKE.

Average Cost.

Ingredients.

	s.	d.
¼ lb. of butter	0	4
6 oz. of flour	0	1
6 oz. of sugar	0	2
4 eggs	0	4
1 lemon	0	1
1 teaspoonful of baking powder	0	0¼
½ a gill of milk	0	0¼
1 oz. of candied peel	0	2
	1	2½

Time, about one hour.

1. Take a clean basin.

2. Beat a quarter of a pound of fresh butter to a cream with

3. Six ounces of pounded and sifted loaf sugar.

4. Grate the rind of a lemon.

5. Mix it with the other things, also

6. The six ounces of flour,

7. In which the baking powder has been well mixed previously.

8. Add to the whole the candied peel cut into small pieces.

9. Beat thoroughly four eggs in half a gill of milk, and mix them in lightly to the other ingredients.

10. Line a cake tin with buttered paper.

11. Put the mixture into it and bake.

No. 48.—SURREY TEA CAKES.

Average Cost.

Ingredients.

	s.	d.
1 lb. of flour	0	2½
½ lb. of butter	0	8
1 gill of milk	0	1
A pinch of salt.		
½ a teaspoonful of baking powder ...	0	0¼
	0	11¾

Time, half an hour.

1. Put one pound of flour into a clean basin.
2. Rub into it half a pound of salt butter,
3. A pinch of salt, and
4. Half a teaspoonful of baking powder.
5. Mix with a little milk to form a stiff paste.
6. Flour a board.
7. Place the paste on it and roll until half an inch in thickness.
8. Cut it into rounds the size of a small plate.
9. Bake on a flat buttered tin.
10. When done, split each one into halves and butter thickly.
11. Cut the cakes into quarters and place in the oven for a few minutes. Send to table *very* hot.

No. 49.—QUEEN'S SPONGE CAKE.

Average Cost.

Ingredients.

		s.	d.
6 eggs	...	0	6
½ lb. of sugar	...	0	2½
½ lb. of flour	...	0	1½
1 lemon	...	0	1
		0	11

Time, three-quarters of an hour.

1. Separate the whites of six eggs from the yolks.

2. For half an hour whisk the whites to a stiff froth.

3. Beat the yolks thoroughly and add them lightly to the whites.

4. Pound and sift half a pound of sugar.

5. Mix it into the eggs and whisk all together for five minutes.

6. Sift half a pound of flour.

7 Stir into the other ingredients with a wooden spoon.

8. Mix the flour in well.

9. Butter a cake tin pretty thickly all over.

10. Scatter a little icing sugar all over the buttered tin.

11. Pour the cake mixture into the tin.

N.B.—The butter used to grease the cake tin should be clarified before being put on, or the paste is likely to stick to the mould.

No. 50.—SMALL SPONGE CAKES.

AVERAGE COST.

Ingredients.

	s.	d.
12 eggs	1	0
1½ lb. of sugar	0	6
2 lemons	0	2
¼ lb. of flour	0	1
	1	9

Time, about half an hour.

1. Beat the yolks of twelve eggs very light.
2. Add to the beaten yolks one pound and a half of finely pounded and sifted loaf sugar.
3. Beat all together for twenty minutes.
4. Beat the whites of twelve eggs to a stiff froth.
5. Work them lightly into the yolks and sugar.
6. Sift four ounces of dry flour.
7. Mix with it the grated rinds of two lemons.
8. Add the flour to the other ingredients.
9. Thoroughly mix all together.
10. Place in small buttered tins.
11. Dust powdered sugar over the cakes before putting them into a hot oven.
12. Leave the oven door a little way open while the sponge cakes are baking.

No. 51.—GINGERBREAD.

Average Cost.

Ingredients.

	s.	d.
1 lb. of flour	0	2½
¼ oz. of ground allspice	0	0¼
¾ lb. of treacle	0	2
½ lb. of butter	0	8
1 oz. of ginger	0	2
3 eggs	0	3
½ a teaspoonful of carbonate of soda	0	0¼
¼ pint of warm milk	0	0½
1 teaspoonful of vinegar.		
½ lb. of coarse sugar	0	1½
	1	8

Time, half an hour.

1. Put the pound of flour into a clean basin.
2. Add to it half a pound of coarse brown sugar.
3. One ounce of ginger, and
4. A quarter of an ounce of allspice.
5. Mix these well together.
6. Cream half a pound of butter.
7. Add three-quarters of a pound of treacle to it.
8. Whisk the eggs well.
9. Dissolve the carbonate of soda in the warm milk.
10. To which add the vinegar.
11. Mix all the ingredients together, and the eggs last of all.
12. Pour the mixture on a floured flat tin, and bake in a good oven.

No. 52.—RUSSIAN WALNUT CAKE.

(Peculiar to the Baltic Provinces.)

AVERAGE COST.

Ingredients.

	s.	d.
10 eggs	0	10
1 lb. of sugar	0	5
2 lb. of walnuts	0	6
¾ of a cup of manna	0	6
1 lemon	0	1
	2	4

Time, about an hour.

1. Beat the yolks of ten eggs with
2. One pound of sugar to a froth.
3. Peel and pound the walnuts.
4. Add them to the yolks and sugar.
5. Grate the peel of one lemon and mix it with the other ingredients.
6. Froth the whites of the eggs and add them last to the mixture.
7. Butter a cake tin with fresh butter.
8. Strew the three-quarters of a cup of manna over the butter in the cake tin.
9. Pour the mixture into it.
10. Bake in an oven the same heat as would be required for bread.
11. Allow the cake *to remain* in the tin after it is baked until it is cold.

N.B.—Manna can be bought by the ounce of any chemist.

No. 53.—LOBSTER MAYONNAISE SANDWICHES.

AVERAGE COST FOR TWENTY PERSONS.

Ingredients.

	s.	d.
1 lobster	2	6
1 tinned loaf	0	5
½ lb. of butter	0	8
1 pint of best Lucca oil	1	0
1 teaspoonful of anchovy sauce	0	0½
3 eggs	0	3
1 lemon	0	1
Chervil leaves		
2 bunches of water-cress		
Cayenne pepper		
White pepper	0	3
A pinch of nutmeg		
A few drops of tarragon vinegar		
½ a mustard-spoonful of Finch's mustard		
	5	2½

1. Take a fine lobster, break the shell and extract the meat.

2. Shred it into pieces.

3. Pour over the shred lobster a thick mayonnaise made as follows :—

4. Stir the yolks of three raw eggs quickly in a basin with a wooden spoon.

5. Add half a teaspoonful of salt, a little cayenne, white pepper, a pinch of grated nutmeg, half a mustard-spoonful of freshly made Finch's mustard, half a teaspoonful of lemon juice, three drops of

tarragon vinegar, and one teaspoonful of anchovy sauce.

6. Stir all together quickly, and

7. Add drop by drop a pint of the very purest olive oil obtainable, stirring all the time it is being dropped in.

8. When the mayonnaise is about to be used stir into it some chopped chervil leaves.

9. Cut some delicate slices of bread and butter.

10. Arrange and spread the lobster and mayonnaise upon the bread and butter.

11. Pluck off the leaves of the water-cress (the stalks must on no account be used).

12. Put the water-cress over the lobster mixture.

13. Place a slice of the bread and butter over that on which the lobster is spread.

14. Press tightly down on to the under slice.

15. Cut into squares of two inches, and serve arranged tastefully on a napkin.

No. 54.—NASTURTIUM LEAVES SANDWICHES.

AVERAGE COST FOR TWENTY PERSONS.

Ingredients.

	s.	d.
1 tinned loaf	0	5
½ a pot of anchovy paste	0	6
½ lb. of butter	0	8
40 nasturtium leaves	0	1
	1	8

1. Cut some thin bread and butter.

2. Spread very sparingly with anchovy paste.

3. Shred some nasturtium leaves and lay on the top of the paste.

4. Place a second piece of bread and butter on the top of the first.

5. Press the two tightly together.

6. Cut into oblong pieces two and a half inches long, and serve.

No. 55.—TOMATO AND SARDINE SANDWICHES.

Average Cost for Twenty Persons.

Ingredients.

	s.	d.
1 tinned loaf	0	5
½ lb. of fresh butter	0	8
1 box of sardines	0	10
Cayenne, Black pepper, Salt	0	1
½ a lemon	0	0½
1 lb. of tomatoes	0	6
	2	6½

1. Cut some slices of thin white bread and butter.

2. Bone and pass ten sardines through a sieve with a piece of butter the size of an egg, well seasoned with cayenne, black pepper, and salt.

3. Spread the mixture upon the bread and butter.

4. Skin one pound of ripe tomatoes.

5. Cut them in thin slices.

6. Squeeze a little lemon juice over each slice.

7. Sprinkle over also a suspicion of castor sugar.

8. Place the slices on the bread and butter over the sardine mixture.

9. Cover with a second piece of bread and butter, and press down firmly on the under one.

10. Cut the sandwiches into rounds with a sharp cutter.

No. 56.—DRIED SALMON SAND-WICHES.

Average Cost for Twenty Persons.

Ingredients.

			s.	d.
1 tinned brown loaf	...	... ...	0	5
½ lb. of fresh butter	..	...	0	8
Cayenne, Salt, Black pepper	...	... ...	0	1
½ a lemon	...	... ...	0	0½
1 bunch of water-cress	...	...	0	1
½ lb. of dried salmon	...	...	1	9
			3	0½

1. Cut some thin slices of brown bread and butter.

2. With a very sharp knife cut some thin slices of boiled dried salmon.

3. Sprinkle with cayenne, black pepper, and salt.

4. Pluck off the leaves of the water-cress and place upon the slices of salmon.

5. Squeeze a little lemon juice over the salmon.

6. Lay the slices upon bread and butter.

7. Cover with a second slice.

8. Cut into squares.

No. 57.—CAVIARE SANDWICHES.

AVERAGE COST FOR TWENTY PERSONS.

Ingredients.

	s.	d.
1 tinned loaf ...	0	5
1 jar of caviare	2	6
½ lb. of butter	0	8
1 lemon ...	0	1
Black pepper and salt	0	0½
	3	8½

1. Cut some slices of bread.
2. Toast on both sides.
3. Take the toast before it is quite cool (but not too hot), and split it down the centre with a fork (a knife is apt to make it heavy).
4. Spread some butter on the soft side of the divided toast, and
5. With a silver knife spread on the top pretty thickly some caviare.
6. Pepper the caviare well, and sprinkle a very little salt upon it.
7. Squeeze a little lemon juice over each slice.
8. Cover the caviare with the second half of the divided toast.
9. Press firmly on to the underneath piece.
10. Cut into two inch squares, and serve.

N.B.—Caviare must on no account be touched with a steel knife. Caviare sold by Tongue, Scale Lane, Hull, is of excellent quality.

These sandwiches must not be prepared long before they are to be used, or they will become tough and leathery.

No. 58.—SHRIMP SANDWICHES.

Average Cost for Twenty Persons.

Ingredients.

	s.	d.
1 pint of shelled shrimps	0	6
½ a salt-spoonful of cayenne } 1 teaspoonful of anchovy sauce } ½ a teaspoonful of lemon juice }	0	1
½ lb. of butter	0	8
1 tinned loaf	0	5
	1	8

1. Pound one pint of shelled shrimps with

2. Half a salt-spoonful of cayenne.

3. One teaspoonful of anchovy sauce.

4. Half a teaspoonful of lemon juice, and salt to taste.

5. Cut some thin white bread and butter.

6. Spread the mixture on it.

7. Cover with a second slice.

8. Press the two pieces firmly together.

9. Cut into sandwiches, and serve.

No. 59.—SALSIFY (OR MOCK OYSTER) SANDWICHES.

AVERAGE COST FOR TWENTY PERSONS.

Ingredients.

	s.	d
1 tinned loaf of brown bread	0	5
3 roots of salsify	0	9
1 wine-glass of vinegar	0	1
¼ pint of cream	0	3
2 teaspoonfuls of anchovy sauce	0	1
Cayenne pepper.		
1 lemon	0	1
½ lb. of butter	0	8
	2	4

1. Take three roots of salsify.
2. Throw them into cold water with
3. A wine-glass of vinegar in it.
4. Leave them in the water for an hour.
5. Boil till tender in well-salted water.
6. Drain and pound with
7. A quarter of a pint of cream.
8. Two teaspoonfuls of anchovy sauce.
9. Season well with cayenne pepper.
10. Cut some slices of thin bread and butter.
11. Spread the mixture pretty thickly upon it.
12. Cover the sandwich, cut into rounds, and serve.

No. 60.—PÂTÉ DE FOIE GRAS SANDWICHES.

AVERAGE COST FOR TWENTY PERSONS.

Ingredients.

	s.	d.
1 jar of Hummel's (Strasbourg) Pâté de Foie Gras	5	0
1 tinned loaf	0	5
½ lb. of butter	0	8
Cayenne and Salt to taste	0	1
Water-cress	0	2
	6	4

1. Cut some delicate bread and butter.

2. Spread thickly upon it some Pâté de Foie Gras.

3. Sprinkle over it some cayenne and salt.

4. Pick off the leaves of the water-cress, and lay them between the sandwich on the Foie Gras.

5. Press down firmly the covering on the pâté, and cut into oblong pieces.

6. Serve piled up on a folded napkin.

N.B.—This Foie Gras can be bought of J. A. Boville, 29A, Upper Gloucester Place, N.W., and is exceptionally delicious.

No. 61.—ASPARAGUS SANDWICHES.

Average Cost.

Ingredients.

	s.	d.
50 heads of asparagus	1	6
1 tinned loaf	0	5
½ lb. of butter	0	8
Mayonnaise sauce, as in No. 53	1	4
	3	11

1. Boil the asparagus in well-salted water till quite tender.

2. Cut off the green heads.

3. Prepare some thick mayonnaise sauce, as directed in No. 53.

4. Put the asparagus heads into it.

5. Spread the whole mixture on the bread and butter.

6. Cover with a second slice, firmly pressed down upon the first.

7. Cut into fanciful shapes, and serve on a folded napkin.

No. 62.—POTTED SALMON SAND-WICHES.

Average Cost.

Ingredients.	s.	d.
1 lb. of salmon	2	0
½ a teaspoonful of pounded cloves	0	1
2 teaspoonfuls of anchovy sauce	0	1
Cayenne and Salt to taste Black pepper	0	0¼
1 teaspoonful of lemon juice	0	0½
½ lb. of butter	0	8
1 tinned loaf	0	5
½ a cucumber	0	6
	3	9¾

1. Pound in a mortar one pound of cold salmon (canned salmon is almost as good as fresh for the purpose).

2. Two ounces of butter.

3. Half a teaspoonful of pounded cloves.

4. Two teaspoonfuls of anchovy sauce.

5. Season highly with cayenne.

6. A teaspoonful of lemon juice.

7. Half a teaspoonful of black pepper.

8. Spread this mixture on thin slices of bread and butter.

9. On the top of which place some strips of very thinly cut cucumber.

10. Press down the second slice of bread and butter firmly on the under one.

11. Cut into small rounds.

12. Serve on a folded napkin, and garnish with water-cress.

No. 63.—MUSHROOM SANDWICHES.

Average Cost for Ten Persons.

Ingredients.

	s.	d.
10 mushrooms	0	6
2 red chillies		
1 teaspoonful of lemon juice	0	0½
Salt }		
½ an onion }	0	1
Cayenne }		
2 ripe tomatoes	0	3
½ oz. of bread crumbs }		
1 gill of milk }	0	1
1 tinned loaf	0	5
½ lb. of butter	0	8
1 egg	0	1
	2	1½

1. Stew ten mushrooms with some
2. Black pepper, a little lemon juice and salt,
3. Two red chillies,
4. One egg,
5. One gill of milk,
6. Two large ripe tomatoes, half an ounce of bread crumbs, and half an onion.
7. When thoroughly done, pass through a sieve.
8. Stand to get cold.
9. Cut some thin bread and butter, and spread with the mixture.
10. Press the top slice down firmly on the under one, and cut into oblong pieces.

No. 64—OLIVE AND ANCHOVY SANDWICHES.

AVERAGE COST FOR SIX PERSONS.

Ingredients.

	s.	d.
12 olives	0	6
3 anchovies	0	3
¼ lb. of butter	0	4
Cayenne	0	0¼
1 tinned loaf	0	2½
	1	3¾

1. Scrape and bone three anchovies.
2. Pound them in a mortar,
3. With cayenne to taste.
4. Stone and finely mince ten olives.
5. Mix them with the anchovies.
6. Cut some slices of very thin bread and butter.
7. Spread with the olive and anchovy mixture.
8. Press a second piece of bread and butter firmly on the top.
9. Cut into oblong pieces, and serve.

No. 65.—EGG AND GHERKIN SANDWICHES.

Average Cost for Ten Persons.

Ingredients.

	s.	d.
5 eggs	0	5
Cayenne and Salt	0	0¼
½ lb. of butter	0	8
1 brown tinned loaf	0	5
2 oz. of gherkins	0	4
	1	10¼

1. Pass the yolks of two eggs through a sieve.

2. Season well with salt, cayenne, and mix in a little butter.

3. Mince the whites of the eggs very fine.

4. Mince the gherkins very fine.

5. Mix the ingredients together.

6. Cut some thin bread and butter.

7. Spread the mixture upon it.

8. Cover with a second slice of bread and butter pressed firmly down upon the first.

9. Cut into pretty shapes, and serve.

No. 66.—COLNBROOK SANDWICHES (EXCELLENT).

Average Cost for Ten Persons.

Ingredients.

	s.	d.
3 oz. of boiled beef	0	1½
Black pepper	0	0¼
½ lb. of butter	0	8
1 tinned loaf	0	5
1 oz. of pickled cabbage	0	2
	1	4¾

1. Pound three ounces of cold boiled beef, half fat and half lean (previously having passed it twice through a mincing machine).

2. Pound a good quantity of black pepper with the meat, and a lump of butter.

3. Spread the mixture on thinly cut bread and butter.

4. Cut some wafer-thin slices of boiled beef.

5. Cut it into strips, and lay it on the potted meat.

6. Then cut thin short strips of pickled cabbage, and lay them on the top of all.

7. Cover with a second slice of bread and butter, well pressed down on the under one. Cut into squares, and serve.

No. 67.—INDIAN HAM SANDWICHES.

Average Cost for Fifteen Persons.

Ingredients.

	s.	d.
¼ lb. of ham	0	3
½ lb. of butter	0	8
1 tinned loaf	0	2½
1½ oz. of Indian chutney	0	2
Cayenne } Chervil }	0	1
	1	4½

1. Pound a quarter of a pound of cooked Yorkshire ham in a mortar (having previously twice run it through a mincing machine, to make the process easier),

2. With a good quantity of cayenne and

3. Three ounces of butter.

4. Cut some thin bread and butter.

5. Spread some of the potted ham upon it.

6. And cover the ham with a thin layer of Indian chutney and a sprinkling of chopped chervil.

7. Place a second piece of bread and butter over the mixture.

8. Press down firmly, and cut into any shape liked.

9. Serve on a folded napkin, and garnish with parsley.

No. 68.—ANCHOVY SANDWICHES (VERY GOOD).

Average Cost for Ten Persons.

Ingredients.

	s.	d.
10 anchovies	0	10
Mustard and cress	0	2
1 tinned brown loaf	0	2½
½ lb. of butter	0	8
5 eggs	0	5
Cayenne.		
	2	3½

1. Wash and bone ten anchovies.
2. Divide into halves, and then cut into short pieces.
3. Hard boil five eggs, shell, and cut into slices.
4. Cut some thin bread and butter.
5. Place the egg slices on it.
6. Sprinkle sparingly with cayenne.
7. Place the anchovies upon the eggs.
8. Chop the mustard and cress, and scatter over the top.
9. Cover the whole with a second slice of bread and butter.
10. Press it down firmly on the under one.
11. Cut into oblong pieces, and
12. Serve on a folded napkin, arranged around a bunch of mustard and cress.

No. 69.—TOMATO SANDWICHES.

AVERAGE COST FOR EIGHT PERSONS.

Ingredients.

	s.	d.
3 tomatoes	0	6
1 egg	0	1
1 onion }		
White pepper }		
Cayenne }		
1 teaspoonful of vinegar }	0	2
1 teaspoonful of anchovy sauce }		
3 drops of tarragon vinegar }		
¼ pint of salad oil	0	3
1 tinned loaf	0	2½
½ lb. of butter	0	8
	1	10½

1. Take three large ripe tomatoes.

2. Cut them in thin slices with a very sharp knife, and dip them in the following mixture.

3. A teaspoonful of anchovy sauce, a little white pepper, one teaspoonful of white vinegar, three drops of tarragon vinegar, one finely minced onion, cayenne and white pepper to taste, as well as a quarter of a pint of purest salad oil poured in drop by drop, stirring all the time.

4. Prepare some slices of thin white bread and butter, lay the tomato thickly on one slice, and cover with another.

5. Press down as firmly as possible, cut into squares, and

6. Serve on a folded napkin, arranged round three or four ripe tomatoes.

No. 70.—THUNDER AND LIGHTNING SANDWICHES (SWEET).

Average Cost for Ten Persons.

Ingredients.

	s.	d.
4 stale milk rolls	0	4
¼ lb. of golden syrup	0	1¼
½ lb. of Devonshire cream	0	8
¼ lb. of butter	0	4
	1	5¼

1. Cut some very thin slices of bread and butter.

2. Spread some golden syrup upon each slice.

3. Cover with a layer of Devonshire cream.

4. Firmly press a second piece of bread and butter upon it.

5. Trim, cut off the crust, round the edges, and serve in rounds.

No. 71.—CLARET CUP.

AVERAGE COST PER QUART.

Ingredients.

	s.	d.
1 bottle of claret	2	0
1 liqueur-glass of curaçoa	0	6
½ a wine-glass of liqueur brandy	0	6
2 bottles of lemonade	0	4
2 bottles of soda water	0	4
3 tablespoonfuls of sifted sugar	0	1
The peel of half a lemon cut *very* thin A large spray of borage	0	1
2 lb. of ice	0	4
	4	2

N.B.—After the other ingredients are mixed, take the sifted sugar and stir in gently just before serving.

No. 72.—CIDER CUP.

Average Cost.

Ingredients.

	s.	d.
1 quart of cider	1	3
½ a wine-glass of liqueur brandy	0	6
½ ,, curaçoa	0	6
½ ,, ginger cordial	0	4
1 ,, sherry	0	6
The peel of ½ a lemon	0	0½
2 lb. of ice	0	4
1 small sprig of mint		
Three or four thin slices of cucumber	0	1
2 bottles of ginger beer	0	4
	3	10½

1. Peel half a lemon very thin.

2. Cut three slices of cucumber.

3. Put these with a small sprig of mint into

4. One quart of cider.

5. Let this stand a quarter of an hour, then remove the lemon peel, cucumber, and mint.

6. Add the other ingredients.

7. And lastly the ginger beer, which must be added immediately before the cup is drunk.

8. When prepared, stand on the ice in a cool place, as, if ice is put into cider cup, it is apt to make it taste flat.

No. 73.—HOCK CUP.

Average Cost.

Ingredients.

	s.	d.
1 bottle of hock	4	0
1 bottle of soda water	0	2
4 lb. of ice	0	8
3 large slices of pineapple	0	6
1 tablespoonful of sifted sugar	0	1
	5	5

No. 74.—CHAMPAGNE CUP.

Average Cost per Quart.

Ingredients.

	s.	d.
1 bottle of champagne	7	6
2 glasses of brown sherry	1	0
1 small glass of liqueur brandy	0	6
1 small glass of curaçoa	0	6
2 bottles of soda water	0	4
2 tablespoonfuls of sifted sugar	0	1
Cucumber peel		
3 lb. of ice	0	6
	10	5

N.B.—The sifted sugar to be stirred in last of all.

No. 75.—SAM WARD KÜMMEL.

AVERAGE COST PER CLARET GLASS.

Ingredients.

	s.	d.
Large claret glass lined with lemon peel ...	0	1
Almost filled with pounded ice ...	0	4
A liqueur-glass of Kümmel poured on the ice	0	6
	0	11

No. 76.—SILVER FIZ.

AVERAGE COST PER SODA WATER GLASS.

Ingredients.

	s.	d.
White of raw egg	0	1
½ lb. of pounded ice	0	1
1 tablespoonful of sifted sugar	0	0½
1 wine-glass of Old Tom	0	4
A bottle of soda water to make the whole into a froth	0	2
	0	8½

No. 77.—ICED COFFEE.

1. Make a quart of strong coffee (using ten ounces of ground coffee) according to directions given for No. 2.

2. Add half a pint of cream, or more, if liked.

3. Three tablespoonfuls of sifted white sugar.

4. Make eight hours before it is required, and stand it in a refrigerator.

5. Ten minutes before serving pour the coffee into a large glass jug in which is a big lump of ice.

No. 78.—ICED TEA AND LEMON.

1. Make some tea according to directions given in No. 1. Let it stand ten minutes.

2. Sugar it slightly and pour it off the leaves.

3. Stand it in a refrigerator for six hours.

4. Serve it in large china bowls, in which float slices of lemon and lumps of ice.

5. Ladle it out of the bowls into glasses as required, taking care to give a slice of lemon and a piece of ice to each person.

No. 79.—LEMON SYRUP.

(Hardly to be distinguished from freshly made lemonade.)

AVERAGE COST PER QUART.

Ingredients.

	s.	d.
1 oz. of citric acid	0	3
1½ oz. of lump sugar	0	0½
2 lemons	0	2
	0	5½

1. Pour a quart of boiling water on the acid and the sugar.

2. Slice the lemons.

3. Pour one pint of boiling water on each lemon.

4. When quite cold mix all together and pour into a bottle ready for use.

N.B.—To make the syrup into lemonade for a party, mix as much of the syrup as suits the taste with fresh spring water in a large glass jug, and float slices of lemon on the top.

No. 80.—LEMONADE.

1 quart

1. Squeeze the juice of four lemons into a big glass jug, avoiding the pulp, as it would make the mixture bitter.
2. Pour a quart of boiling water upon the juice.
3. Sweeten to taste.
4. Stand to get cool (at least ten hours).
5. Just before serving float some very thinly cut lemon peel in the jug and put in lumps of ice.

No. 81.—SAMSON.

Average Cost per Two Quarts.

Ingredients.

	s.	*d.*
1 bottle of claret	2	0
1 bottle of champagne	7	6
2 bottles of soda water	0	4
1 wine-glass of sherry	0	6
6 strawberries	0	1
3 lb. of ice	0	6
4 tablespoonfuls of sifted sugar	0	0½
	10	11½

N.B.—In all cups and cooling drinks where sugar is used, it must be stirred in gently just before the cup is served, and will be found to impart a smooth creaminess that cannot otherwise be obtained. The sugar used should be pounded and finely sifted "lump."

PRINTED BY WILLIAM CLOWES AND SONS, LIMITED,
LONDON AND BECCLES.

BY MISS HOOPER.

Little Dinners: How to Serve them with Elegance and Economy. Twentieth Edition. Crown 8vo, 2s. 6d.

Cookery for Invalids, Persons of Delicate Digestion, and Children. Fifth Edition. Crown 8vo, 2s. 6d.

Every-Day Meals. Being Economical and Wholesome Receipts for Breakfast, Luncheon, and Supper. Sixth Edition. Crown 8vo, 2s. 6d.

BY MADAME DE JONCOURT.

Wholesome Cookery. Third Edition. Crown 8vo, 3s. 6d.

LONDON: KEGAN PAUL, TRENCH & CO.